People of the Bible

The Bible through stories and pictures

David and Goliath

Copyright © in this format Belitha Press Ltd., 1985

Text copyright © Catherine Storr 1985

Illustrations copyright © Chris Molan 1985

Art Director: Treld Bicknell

First published in the United States of America 1985
by Raintree Publishers Limited Partnership
310 West Wisconsin Avenue, Milwaukee, Wisconsin 53203
in association with Belitha Press Ltd., London.

Conceived, designed and produced by Belitha Press Ltd.,
2 Beresford Terrace, London N5 2DH

ISBN 0-8172-1995-1 (U.S.A.)

Library of Congress Cataloging in Publication Data

Storr, Catherine.
  David and Goliath.

  (People of the Bible)
  Summary: A shepherd boy leads the Israelites to
victory by killing the giant leader of the opposing army.
    1. David, King of Israel—Juvenile literature.
2. Goliath (Biblical giant)—Juvenile literature.
[1. David, King of Israel. 2. Goliath (Biblical
giant) 3. Bible stories—O.T.] I. Title.
II. Series.
BS580.D3S69   1984   222′.4309505   84-18138

ISBN 0-8172-1995-1

First published in Great Britain 1985
by Franklin Watts Ltd.,
12a Golden Square, London W1

Printed in The United States of America.

891011121314 97 96 95 94 93 92 91

David and Goliath

Retold by Catherine Storr
Pictures by Chris Molan

Raintree Childrens Books
Milwaukee
Belitha Press Limited • London

One day, God spoke to Samuel, the High Priest. He said, "Saul, the King of Israel, does not obey my commandments. I am going to choose another king to rule instead of him.

Go on a journey into the country. Near
Bethlehem you will find a man called Jesse.
I have chosen a new king from among his
sons."

Samuel said, "Lord God, how can I do this?
If Saul hears of my journey, he will kill me."

God said, "Take an animal with you, and tell people that you are going to make a sacrifice to the Lord."

The next day, Samuel journeyed toward Bethlehem. When the people from the town saw him, they were troubled. They asked, "Do you come in peace?"

Samuel said, "I come in peace, to make a sacrifice to the Lord."

He called Jesse and his sons to the sacrifice.
When he saw Eliab, the oldest, he said, "This
must be the man I have come to find."

But God said, "No. This is not the right
man."

Next, Samuel saw Abinadab, but he was not the man God had chosen.

Then Jesse brought another son, Shammah, and all the sons in his house for Samuel to see. But not one was the right one.

Samuel asked, "Have you no more sons?"
Jesse said, "There is one more, the youngest.
He is out on the hills tending the sheep."
Samuel said, "Send for him."

Jesse sent up to the hills, and David, his youngest son, came down. He was young and handsome to look at.

When Samuel saw him, he knew that this was the boy God had chosen. He took a horn of oil and anointed David as the man who would one day be King of Israel.

It happened that at this time Saul was troubled by an evil spirit. He became very sad and miserable, and he could not sleep.

His servants said, "A cunning player on the harp would drive away this evil spirit, and you would feel better."

Saul said, "Very well. Find me such a man."

A servant said, "One of Jesse's sons plays the harp, and he is very brave and very good looking."

Saul sent messengers to Jesse to ask that
David should come down to him. When Jesse
heard the message, he sent bread and wine and
a kid with David as gifts for King Saul.

As soon as Saul saw David, he loved him.
David played the harp, and his music calmed
Saul. The evil spirit left him.

A great war was being fought between the Israelites and the Philistines. The two armies were encamped on two mountains on opposite sides of a valley.

One of the Philistines was a giant called Goliath. He was very tall and immensely strong.

He wore armor of brass, and his spear was as thick as a young tree. He called out to the Israelites, "Send out a man to fight me in single combat!"

But the Israelites were afraid. No one would go out to fight Goliath.

17

Jesse's three oldest sons were in the army, fighting with Saul against the Philistines. One day, Jesse said to David, "Take this measure of corn and these ten loaves. Go to the camp

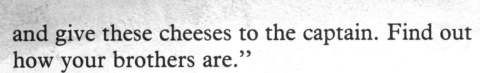

and give these cheeses to the captain. Find out how your brothers are."

Early the next morning David went to the camp. He heard Goliath shouting across the valley, and he asked his brothers, "What reward is there for the man who will go out to fight this roaring giant?"

David's oldest brother was angry, and said,
"Why didn't you stay in the hills with your
sheep? You just came down here to see the
battle."

David asked other people about Goliath.

Saul heard that a young man was saying that
someone should fight Goliath. He sent for
David, and David said to him, "I will go out
and fight this Philistine."

Saul said, "You can't fight Goliath. He has been fighting for years, and you are only a boy."

David said, "For a long time I have been guarding my father's sheep. Once a lion took a lamb, but I made him drop it out of his mouth. Then I took him by the beard and killed him. I know that I can kill this Philistine who is defying the army of the living God."

When he heard that, Saul said, "Go, then, and God go with you." He gave David his own armor, a brass helmet, a coat of mail, and a sword.

But David said, "I have never fought in armor. I think I would do better without it."

He took it off, and went to the battlefield to meet Goliath. On his way, David stopped to pick up some stones.

As soon as Goliath saw the young David, he said, "Am I a dog, that you come to fight me without a sword, with only sticks?

"Come nearer, and I will kill you, and feed your body to the fowls of the air and to the beasts of the field."

David said, "You come to fight me with a sword and a spear, but I come in the name of the Lord God." Then he put a stone into a sling and hurled it at Goliath. It hit the Philistine on the forehead, so that he fell on his face on the earth.

David ran up and stood on
Goliath's body. He took Goliath's
sword and cut off the giant's head.
    Then the Israelite army stood
up and shouted. They chased the
Philistine army up the valley as
far as the gates of Ekron.

After the battle, Abner, the Israelite captain, brought David before Saul in Jerusalem. David had with him Goliath's head and his armor. Saul asked David, "Whose son are you, young man?" David said, "I am the son of Jesse of Bethlehem."

One of Saul's sons, called Jonathan, saw how handsome and brave David was. He knew then that he would love this young man as if he were his brother.

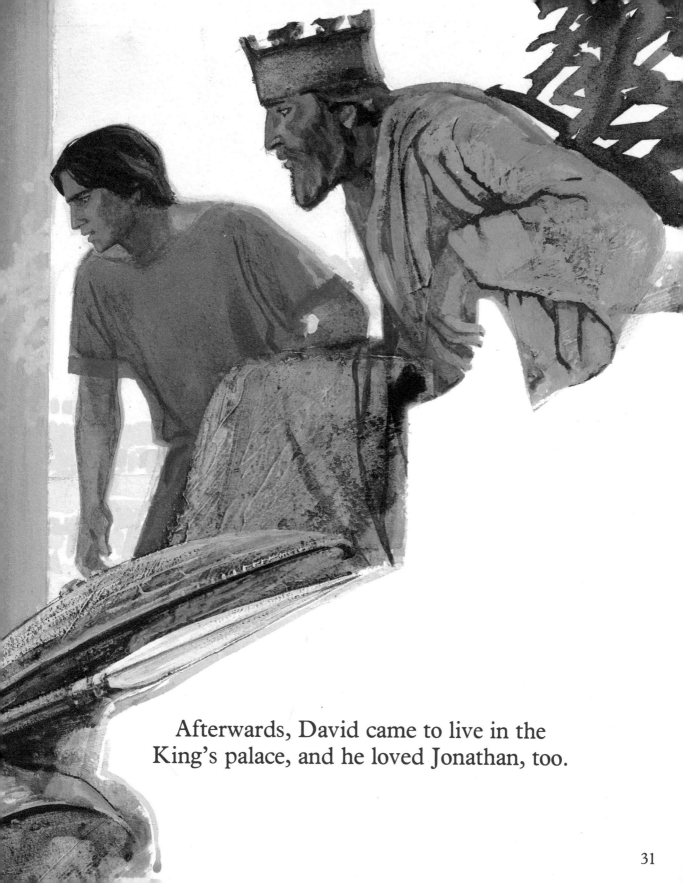

Afterwards, David came to live in the King's palace, and he loved Jonathan, too.

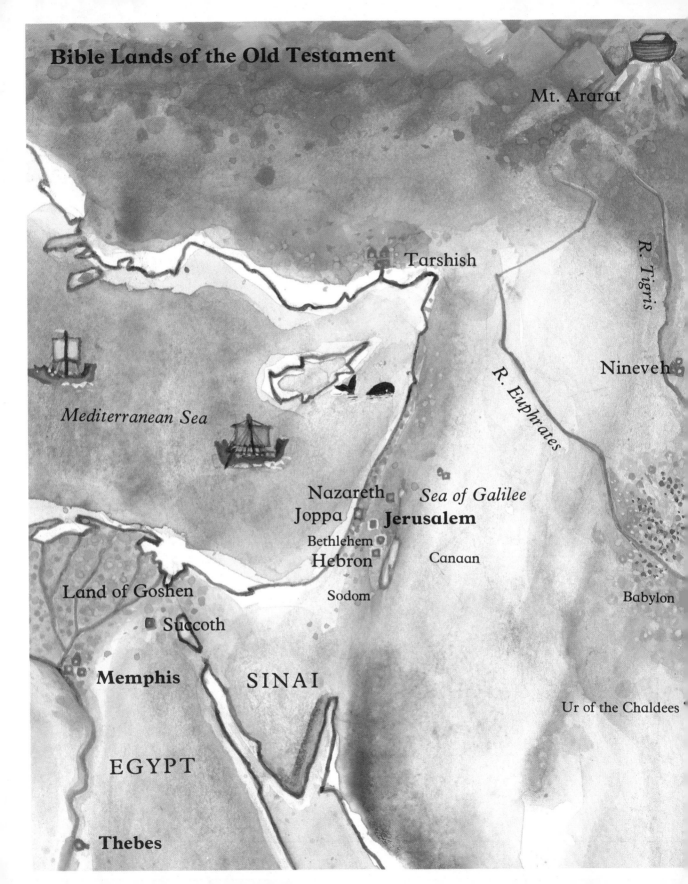

Bible Lands of the Old Testament

Mt. Ararat

Tarshish

R. Tigris

Nineveh

Mediterranean Sea

R. Euphrates

Nazareth *Sea of Galilee*

Joppa **Jerusalem**

Bethlehem

Hebron Canaan

Sodom

Babylon

Land of Goshen

Succoth

Ur of the Chaldees

Memphis

SINAI

EGYPT

Thebes